Drum the Double Sun

Algoems

Drum the Double Sun

Algoems

Daniel Manuel Mendoza

MADVILLE
PUBLISHING

LAKE DALLAS, TEXAS

FIRST EDITION

Requests for permission to reprint or reuse material
from this work should be sent to:

Permissions
Madville Publishing
PO Box 358
Lake Dallas, TX 75065

Author Photo: Daniel Manuel Mendoza
Cover Art & Design: Luis Corpus

ISBN: 978-1-963695-19-9 paperback
978-1-963695-20-5 ebook
Library of Congress Control Number: 2024940808

for Cayetano and Everett

Contents

Once by the Mexica Lily

"So, you want to be
A poet?"
Salamander inquired.

I said, "Yes, if
You'll inspire."

And with a brush
Of its spiraled hand
There set fire

To all other things
I had ever desired.

Barreling through the fleshed

Hallways of memory, I will stand
Wide eyed with you in that old golden
Dusk of South Texas—Great Sky
Of days. We'll laugh as empty
Bottles of Miller High Life clank
One against the other in Frank's Café,
Or we'll toss cigarette butts
Into a swimming pool filled with trash
At the old motel on Highway 16 waiting
For the 460 Ford thundering from Roma.
O! In that silent sun of morning
We'll break tires to make money
For lunch on old engine blocks.
We'll skip out of classrooms
To smoke dugouts in drain ditches
Dusty with July. We'll talk of Big Bob
And allow his wisdom and laughter
To become a permanence beyond long
Memory death. And sing his name auric
From our lips slow and warm
Like mesquite honey, mysterious,
And always true. Huddling into old Z28s
And F-150s the world freer
Beyond our birth more magical,
Or we'll love in the back of rusted
Farm truck beds, the sweet smell
Of buffalo grass tinged by the afternoon's
Warming. We'll sneak up gracelit staircases
And pull the moth-eaten curtains to stare
Down at the Y from the abandoned Viggo Hotel,
Or rummage the old buildings of downtown,
Or the rusted boxcars in old Hebbronville.
It'll all be no matter with cigarettes and beer,
Because there is no other way to bypass
One's birth or to walk through the human corridor.

I was rusted birth nickel in the street seam

My pop pieced flesh from the highway
A teamster Adam of brake grease and speed
Diesel trunk and murderous heels
Through the salt snow road
Of East Chicago, Cline Avenue,
Hessville and Gary, Indiana.

My morale, my yarn unless divided
Carry me, carry me, to the soot
Outside the door.
My morale, my yarn unless divided
Carry me, carry me
To the tire, the hammer, the lore.

Learned to spit the blood of sacrifice
And with hungry fingers I picked
The vine of days my genesis in tire
Iron and made dollars from marijuana
Shelling-shifting the day's death hours
Of a workman's void hungry as I take.

My morale, my yarn unless divided
Carry me, carry me, to the soot
Outside the door.
My morale, my yarn unless divided
Carry me, carry me
To the tire, the hammer, the lore.

Into the sweetened flesh
Of sun-kissed South Texas girls
Waiting cuntsoft in their pillow-eyed
Meander where the luckiest
Of youth and I reach beyond
The return, shaping radiated
And stinking of the brush country

Sun smitten birthing blind
Against the turning chapter
In the heat of this our South Texas.

Mint me among

The mesquite
Along 359, allow
The goodmen
The callow eyes
Of morale.

Give me this
Hour, and if when
The throes deny
Me, a Man stained
And maniacal,
Show them the sinew
Of my tire-worked
Forearms, the arthritic
Hands wrenched
From working
A good day's

Death.

How many ragged, humid dawns

Have you woken damp swollen
And rust hardened, your hands
Calloused against the knees
Of day? In that dark, groan-empty
House, to turn water for the tendoned
Path, followed with coffee, bread,
Bacon, and smoke. They'll be dollars
From irons prying tires from wheels.

81-year-old knuckles bleeding
Fleshed nickel into black tubs
For a 24-year-old kid smoking
A menthol waiting in fewer
Multitudes to get on Highway 359 again.

You won't sketch or precedent
A chorus to patch together
The splendorous day for those
Skeptic poets of thinking.

Those fools, you say, can save themselves
With their whiskey-warm heaving.

We Were Fools

Across your eye
Like a blur. We were
Just young, we were just
Ample, and I did not know
These things when they cut
Like smooth birch swift
In the nose, burning like gasoline.
Across the horizon Highway 16
Goes like a sad song
That doesn't mean anymore.
So see you in the alphabet ruin
You always were. Your heart
Behind the damp muscle that
Left all of us back there.
In dreams the world promised
Success, remember? I know
You fantasy-hearted, still
A jack in the shade:
Verily, verily I say unto you
Like a corn of wheat
You've long gone to run
The void and sever the line
Of our curdled dusk.

What I have seen

Were no miracles.
No product angel-like
Comforting my world.
What I have seen
In the late spring
As I zoomed the outskirts
Of Hebbronville, Highway 16,
Were the firewheels and phlox
In the early morning.

Joy of Oblivion

I was ravenous once
Languishing the hot breeze
Of Highway 16, opulent
And reckless before
We became these storied
Skeletons of Babylon.

Of marijuana backyards,
Of moist, hot Mexican thighs,
Of smoky glass pipes.

Does the glory remain still?

A silhouetted history of parking
Lots and old houses junked
With the long, curdled hours of day.

And of the faces and streets,
And the tattooed tongues, and suicide
Flowers of Friday, and alcoholic
schemes: All those relentless lifetimes
Make my heart pulse like a bomb:

Tick
Tock

BOOM!

My youth stood suspended

On sawhorses. Below the red ruin
Of siblings, umbilical chords,
And assembled sadness where women
Bore down on me. Far off
My father dug a hole for time,
A westward forum for the absence
That would divide us beyond my adolescence.

When in my youth

I looked about America
From atop my father's
Shoulders and understood
Its makings by his laughter
And its freedom by his forearms
Soiled with engine grease.

Now I sit near the culmination
Of another dark year
Longing to understand
When to laugh or cry
At the comedy and tragedy
Of it all: this bright sadness,
The necessity of realization,
The impersonal perpetuations
Of duty, and the posture
Of Hestian sincerity.

Gassed by the pushcart of dumbfoundment,

When in my youth
I looked about America
From atop my father's
Shoulders and understood.

A Western Tragedy

In a dream my word became older than Rome.
I prayed the end of this cold empire, the end
Of They who heralded the Evangelic fatmen
Of Washington, the end of They who cursed
The eternity of the Line.

Scarlet laments unshackled, I walked
This tattered democracy joining the quaint-hearted
And amorous, cavaliering the curious remains
Of day.

From my eyes lifetimes passed, and I visaged
A myriad great truths and saw all that I loved
In bed and dead in America.

What great visage of ages

Has man erected upon Idea.
O! Towering concrete
Steel phallics of his Godhood.
And lo! He has never
But lent a fleshed son,
Some dozen dumb seers
Gassed in dumbfoundment.
Pray the Word, Fatman!
Pray the Word!
For amidst this chaos
Of humanity there lie
Only one you would kill
For—though it be many names
Surely you know the only one?

Modern Man

I have found virtue
In the toils of life:
The spiritus of poetry
The legs of the working women
And tequila of the trodden.

What amount of fears
Has humanity suffered?
Cowered solemn as a dog
In the windings of the night.

I have found virtue
In the spoils of life:
The rhythm of poem
The smirk of the working women
And callous of the trodden.

What calamity of want
Has humanity bothered?
Rigorous movement as a fog
In the windings of the night.

I have found virtue
In the toils of life:
The vanity of poetics
The crown of the working women
The footsteps of the trodden.

What protest of morals
Has humanity begrudged?
Indifferent as a loosed feather
In the windings of the night.

Yes, as just another
I have found virtue
In the windings of the night.

Philosophers

For theatres of loneliness
Where bitter hearts waver
Among hallowed chests.

There above wavering lights
A minstrel fly buzzes
Unaware of the presence
Its fluttering shell abates.

Whereby the anxious species
Listens through dry ribs
For a voice, a morning logic
Crowned by the heavens.

They listen grace-driven
By their ignorance.

DC in Spring (for Kas)

Drowsy on the Amtrak out
Of Philadelphia's 30th Street, I
Image you in the capital city,
Intent against the halls of Justice
And Neptune. Your bright eyes
Over the Library of Congress.

What love, what resolve,
Laughter, and tragedy, Kas,
Have you found in this
Cold American city?

The conductor at Union Station
Tells us we've arrived, and so I
Walk out and onto DC to see
You finally, the miles between
My South Texas, to your east coast
To talk, talk, talk with you
About our shared Midwest, our winter
birth, and our sadness, and the red
Bracelet hugging at your wrist.

My fear of sleep

Brought on the drug-addled
Eye of Memory and the invited
Soul to nightlong schemes.

By myself I sat in the warm
Meander of summer as the moon
Skirted in the Rio Grande Valley
Sky silent, drunken, back-tired
Until the lullaby of streetlights went
Out, out, out, knowing my life
A scene of madwomen and dope-scheme.

So ever on I cherished
The shore of South Padre Island
In the morning and the wants
Of estuary in the indigo of twilight.

Estelle Almée

Anon!

She came
And suddenly!

Had I the tenderness

Of some Goodman's palm
I'd deliver you from the sad curiosities
Of your circumstance. I'd deliver you
From the gilded grace of that Mexica
Catholic death dance. But you contain
The copal glass and I hesitate afraid
To commune at your bed.
Ditching my grace in the rain
False squinting to what tomorrow leans.

Having stood on the bright blanched
Sediment of a Hi-Fi world, having spirited
Through the center of this generation's
Medicinal truth, I'd developed a Novembered
Heart pulling the ears of a rainy day.
And so retraced the battered circumstance
Of this balladed genocide with a sink and stove chest

I became Adam's only son. Dreaming in ragtime—
I became the golden pisser shockwaltzing
The asphodel in an emerald streetcrown.

Begging some Sunday pigeon to enrapture me.

Poem for the May City

I have petitioned the alcoholic day
With a manic hissing under the autochtonic May.
The Valley and its old terrors story and cry;
They grow anxious and red as Metzli's eye.
Oblivion and peril and so my speech stutters
The inevitable mystery of love and carrion.
I have petitioned the alcoholic day
With a tragic hissing under the psalm of May,
Ask Persephone, the nuptialed prey,
Where one wells for warmth in this suicide parade.
I have petitioned the alcoholic day
With beryl stone eyes and the tattoo tongue of May.

Birthday Poem 2 a.m.

The flux of sirens
And flash of lights
Pass on beyond
The drawn curtains
Of apartment windows
McAllen 2 a.m.

Some lazy voice muses
An unconscious cry.

While another walks alone
Like some fat god.

East Chicago Polyptych I

Your eyes the jade palace
Of nurses and gangsters
Of East Chicago.
And Gary is rich
With Catholic masses
And quaint cemeteries.
At your window
Off Northcote Avenue
We smoked the laced
Cigarette, then I watched
You undress under the indigo
Sky of evening. Arms open,
You unmasked drug-addled me
And plucked my Capricorn heart.

East Chicago Polyptych II

Your Puerto Rican hands golden
As a dream caduceus held me close
Like the sparrows of St. Francis.
And I knowing nothing kinder
Gave you mine, arthritic hands
Like a child syllabled and sunned
As Fatima. We talked the poetry
Of Blake and the Zapotecs. We talked
Of the revolving circumstance
Of the Catholic soul, until the waitress
Gave us the tab and we stumbled
Along Carroll Street lisping alcoholic
At the Midwestern stars.

East Chicago Polyptych III

The snow came down
Silver as fountain head.
We walked the blocks
Down Northcote to your
Bedroom and with our evening
Eyes stared at one another
And kissed until my heart
And your heart warmed again.

Where is life, Jessica? And what
Is poetry? The golden hand of Five Flower?
An attempt at songs we used to know?

Love me until we both collapse
Into the laughing sickness and cry
With our hearts flowered purple as prophecy—
The sharp ecstasy of January on my forehead.

East Chicago Polyptych IV

Winter hues gone, so you sleep
The silvered slumber of Citlalli.
Dream throated, but long
Hours ago you clasped
At my dark temples
With your cold hands
Under the slow snow
Of East Chicago. You said
You loved me, Jessica. I said
Your head's not right. Tempest,
Tempesta, tempest of Teyollia
And the quainthood of our blood
February. These city streets weighted
In loss and the choked promises
Of the past. We hold hands now only
To pass the time—you're nauseous,
I'm angry, together groping
For the truth of a life lost.

Love Poem

What Mexican grace
Rendered the supple
Circumference
Of your breasts?

You put my finger
There to summon
The wet of our sin.

On Tacca's Dido

I image you
In dreams gowned
To fate about:
Against the parade
Of clichés
The choked measure
Of pathos. This life,
A sublime reality
And you with ecstasy
In your spine,
Your scabbed hands
Cowering an empty
Stomach, awake
Three days.

Moyolacocqueh

Had she known
It was those hip notions
Pulling, pulling, pulling
Me from my sorrowments,

What then?
Of the laced cigarette
And her turquoise antiquity?

Had her eyes seen
That it was really only me
Goat-footed Pan begging
At her sunned apples
Under the copal dawn:

Would she cradle me again?

On Cline Avenue

There were peaches in her garden—
Shimmering golden, yet green.
They always hung close to the tree—
Resilient, so as to never fall.

Long I wondered
How was it that they would rot?

Independence Day

I shot right through
The center of the muscled
Caverns of her throat,
So came my syrupy sword.
And with the Oread eyes
Of Echo, she smiled.

The pearl now loosed
From her nape, she held
The impossible hammer

Ready to devour me again
With her Cithaeron tongue.

Interiors of Summer

I think of you now
Laughing under the linen
Of our azure afternoon.
Not resisting my desire,
Desire of your thighs,
The July desire of your lips,
And the cosmic eyes
Of your generation,
August eyes that strike
Like gallant cherries—
Youthful to outline
And holy as your hips
In that summered day.

Falser Delights

In a dream
What could you
Do to me?

Beneath
The brown lake
In Zapata, I asked
You once about
The smallest point:
Glorious you answered,
"The equinox!"

Our noses gunning
With Easter's appetite.

Whiskey Daisy

A blush
Brightened
Her eyes
Flooded down
To her chest
Honey sweet
As bourbon.

Anima at the Palace of Butterflies

Had I defied time
Like the perpetual prism
Of the mime,
I'd have found you
Long ago. Spirit
Of my flesh
To your flesh
Spirit spiritus
Ours.

Your curved body
Jove drawn under
The yellow
Balcony light.

In a dream
We were attic
Creatures, tongue
Twined, piercing
Through genesis
And the wise.

Tell me again
How fate rendered
The purple circumference
Of our vernal hour?

Tell me again
Of the myrtle birds
And the inevitable
Salmacis knot
That will soonest
Bind us?

Paradise and Eggs

There was her summer dress and her brown eyes.
The dominance of her Italian nose and Southside heritage:
They considered her an object.

Once at Washington Park she confessed how
She considered me a timepiece of ignorance.

Early Aughts American Tryptic I

Talked, talked, talked in warm truckers' cabs
Reeking of sleep and cigarettes. Hitched and slept
Under the big spring sky. A week to the day, back
Home Cindy buried her chocolate lab under
The front porch. Whopper Tony looking for his daughter
In Seattle, showed me his perfect polaroid just in case.
San Antonio, Denver, Billings, Portland, no place
And all of us: a generation of invisible children.

Early Aughts American Tryptic II

I was too drunk, so Victoria helped
me to the tent. The stars strange then
At that early hour. "Vision proud," she said.
The Perseids at two in the morning.
Thinking of a good life and the last
Night we worked the fair she scoffed:
"This blood's not the end of it all." Mark
Passed out warm between us, so shared
a bottle of MD and whispered
About saving money for a small house.

Early Aughts American Tryptic III

The earth rattled when Father John fell,
His whole side ragged and muddy.
Sister Lisa barked, then scuttled her little feet
Over before I could and mourned. His body
Reeking of rain and earth, the whole lot of us:
The sequoia, the dogs, us, and all else a laboring
Tribe spanning generations of life: the slow
Gesture toward death. It was a gray winter,
After all, and now with the old blue heeler
Gone, the evenings would become more dreary.

Victims in Demand

That hour turned zero
Burns at my spirit hearth,
Black pinned and heavy.
So I lay it down
Amid the scattered sacraments
Of my self—somnolent and marrowed.

Where is the yellow bird donned
With the brass legs of staving
And you on the hotel balcony
Smoking the long cigarette of memory?

Sit with me at the kitchen table,
That fine instrument of crisis,
Where our love became framed
In miscellany and murmur
And our hearts turned to a slow meditation
Languid as the drugged muse of January.

Wisejack Reaching

And what my throat
Mistaked for truth
Became the pancake
Soil that birthed
A hollow howl.
So when 15 years ago
I damned my mother
For the poverty
Of my heart
And the clemency
Of bright circumspection,
No one came to answer me—
Nothing gifted. A moment
Of desire, brought only
A copper pot with bone splinters.
So I loosed my consciousness
And placed a red bulb
Upon my nose and laughed
As my skeleton pose
Became a wisejack reaching.

Blood Under Wood

If it's you I keep
Returning to on days
Like these when the gruel
Of wisdom is locked,
Spooled in cabinets of desire,
When the shadowy membrane
Of suitcases and determination
Flood the newspaper plausibility
Of wet eyes, bending toward poetic
Rhythm: I became jealous,
Splitting the innumerable: shaving
Golgotha's holy firmament.
But you come back, haunting
Upside down to profligate
The vaindrift favor.

In a dream, in a dream the hairy leg of a spider pushes a gas pedal
And moon-hooved Mnetha drowns all images that beg significance.

Moment House

All the places that provided
No coincidence or irony,
All the cardboard suitcases
And Hostel Fish ruminations,
All the poetry, of course.

Stopped on Larimer Street,
Denver, for a cigarette and squinted
At the jasper clouds, George,

Where is the heart that led my body
To desire, unperturbed by television events?

Cay and Rett at the Frio River

Their voices called out amid the Frio River
Trill of evening July, so language became
A flowing thing, and all those yards away
They two together settled on the big granite
Slab, laid about their boyhood triumph:
A leopard frog, a flashlight, and some twisted cypress,
This together the summer could not contain them.

Watch the poets

Knock about
The mechanics
Of the masters
Tracing
The narrow
Circumference
Of an empty bottle:

Empty.

There is not sage

Enough to heal
The poets

Of their wicked,
Wicked repose.

They exist
Loose in
Abstraction,
In digression.

Lofty poets

Who romanticize
Peddling words
Ornate, not wise,

Shall be
Condemned
To an eternity
Of their very
Poetry before
Their eyes.

Red Dot

In the echo
Heart waltz
Of time
I've gazed
Through
The gauze
Of viper sweet
Girls and winners
Of the world
Who with cavities
Of belief gifted
Me articles of truth
For which I played
Too long,
And pondering
Just how I felt
I lamented
The eternal sadness
And the futility
Of remembrance.

Man

Have you
Reckoned
Enough,

The battles
And stages
Of the world?

Drum the double sun

Of May City and song
Her pursed lips against
The theatre of August.

Cilla of the Rio Grande Valley
Upturns her head to the sun.
Bright eyes sublime and
Almond as Aquarius.

St. Catherine of Genoa

Grace you!
Grace you!
And this
Blue divine,
Slow contemplation

Flashlight Gravity House

Without you I meander
The main street and sculptured avenues
In helpless singularity longing
A temporal kind of sleep
That only one Shakespearean
Maid could've wrought.
And of course I lack
Certain sober qualities,
But let me tell you this:
At night I lie alone
In a bayless city listening
To the cement hum
Of automobiles on University
Drive and gather my world
Has become a slow struggle
Of bemused faces and paradoxical
Philosophies. I wake to car horns,
Brakes screeching, freshman pigeons
Of laughter. I wake to garbage
Trucks, fire engines,
Every neighbor's door slamming.

I tell you, H, this distance
The ocean and poetry
between you and me
Is undoubtedly a turbulent one.

O!
In the morning when I gather my things,
In the afternoon when I sit absent hollow in Central Station,
In the evening when I walk the university quad:

It's you!
It's you!
So like the clamorheart of gravity:
It's you!

God is

The empty farm
Truck running

Slow along
The night avenue
Of May City.

H

The notes
Of your voice
Soak my heart:
Whole, poxed
Like a chicken
Put to boil.

A Smash of Doves

I jewel your name
At the yellow post
Light 16th Street

My heart is heavy
As a smash of doves.

Allie knocked

On the door.
Creeped down
Hugging flesh
Her orphaned
Stomach: "My
Back hurts,
I can't keep,
You know?"

Soren Pessoa
Made a call,
She stared
At the ceiling
Rubbing
The buzzer

Sleep to La Luz,
Woke to the garbage
Truck, broke
Pessoa's toenail
The way
She pushed
The door in.

"The gas station
On University."

Half-eight
And MD,
Snarled
As a manged
Dog that cold,
Cold feeling
Nose numb
Happiness of
Gary, Indiana.

Quickdraw

Look!
The marigold sun
Scouring
       Euripides' chin.

Tomorrow
      It'll heave
            Out

The universal contempt.

Let me into the hives

Of your heart.
Piercing
The whisper
Of your gestured
Yarn.

To know
Your eyes
Not a mask

And hold
Your hand
Close amid
The artifice
Of this age.

I petition
The errant muse,
Eye-hallowed
And dreamed.

To know
Your body
Not a mask

O! I am
Carnal-laic
And mad.

Allow me
The August bird
Of your hydromancy.

Allow me
The vast exaltation
Of your body.

O! I am rhapsodic
As the altar-ancient,
Sick of ennui.

Roman Black Garb

In Hellshire I once acquainted
The vomited she-saint of Mercury,

And with a harlequin's tongue
I gained her fancy.

Strawberry Blonde Pose

With fugitive resentment
The gunner clasped
The piece, her teeth
Jawing dawn's repose.

Cocked and addled
Soren Pessoa played the peasant
Redeemer and looked her
Eye on eye: "Through highway
Spring and fanciful engagements,
I've loved you."

"You don't love me. Can you
Ever love me?"

When unsheathed
The quickknife from his peacoat,
The .45 whistled the nickel
Swoon of an antique flute.

A Modern Poem

There are streetlight phantoms
On Austin Avenue, downtown McAllen
That walk with bells on their ankles.
Stoned, imperious princesses

And all the young dudes
In their new colors
Long for a solid fix
Of clean coke and
The clutched legs
Of a drunk Mexican girl.

"Understand there is Love,
And then,
There are those other things
That grace about lightly.
Like daydreams in twilight—

Know these things,"

Pessoa professed sharply.

Shadow Psalm

Radiant heart, don't be a sad heart
In your summer age, Cayetano.
Elicit the sun, bright Apollo
Be forthright in your dream canto:
Faith in your purpose, upright
In your gait, steady as sharp-
Tongued Pan. Don't mind the hours,
Or minutes, or dregs of day.
But mind your shadow, always,
Mind it more than the flight
Of your golden wings.

The Blood Heart and the Golden

What's more, can the blood heart
Blush the merry one golden?

What's more, can the dogs trample
The dove flock of September?

What's more, once it's all done and over
Look yon feverish Virgil at the harbor.

No more, no more,
So sung bright Aries' son.

No more of that blood heart
No more of that golden.

No more of those dogs
No more of those doves.

No more, my bright sons,
Now that it's over.

Mirror Psalm

Sometimes I wonder you
Dionysus' son, your head
Crowned with curls and eyes
Brown as seasoned mesquite.

You've a barrel chest
Like my father, Everett,
And a night whim long
Like your mother's.

Soonest now, boy,
You'll be a young man
And desire to trample
The word that you honor.

But mark time to know
Your self in the mirror
From your self in your father.

Wil and I

Late day
5 p.m.
Wil and I
Gather nails
And a small mallet
For a wire fence.

Buddha chases
His shadow
At dawn.

Wil drives
The posera
Into hard soil;
I gather metal
Ties for the fastening
Of the 8x4s.

Buddha rubs
His belly
On the ground.

Wil and I
Sit inside
For sliced watermelon
And cucumbers grown
Some yards away.

The sun sets
Orange over
The Rio Grande
Valley.

Visions

The Rio Grande Valley is beauty
With fruit and marijuana:
My body consists of both.

There are sun-kissed children
Who run down the dunes
Of South Padre Island
As sun sets in early spring.

Occurrence at a South Texas Ranch

So the body
Borrowed the knife,
But it was only
A consequence
To transcendence.

Tell me, after
The machete

Were you
Neither wild
Nor flowered?

Mexica Instant

Hit me easy
With the ecstasy
Of Mexican reverie.

The arroyo
Brings the feeling
Of springtime love,

The indigo sky
A vision
Of Mexico's glory.

For Dad

Off bustling Highway 359
Is my dad's auto garage.
Outside he eats lunch
Atop an old engine block.

Up high above him
The November sun shines warm.
A brown puppy runs from underneath
A blue pickup truck and rests his chin
Upon his dirty work boots.

Dad looks up and gives me
An ancient hip smile.

Acknowledgments

Earlier versions of "Wil and I," "Occurrence at a South Texas Ranch," "Visions," and "For Dad" appear in the chapbook *Algoems* (The Raving Press, 2007).

I would be nowhere without three individuals: Roberto Gutierrez, Eric Miles Williamson, and Wilbert Martin, whose conversation helped me through the difficulties of writing and living. I owe a great debt to Kim Davis, Linda Parsons, and everyone at Madville Publishing for their indispensable help.

About the Author

Daniel Manuel Mendoza was raised in Hammond, Indiana, and Hebbronville, Texas. He is a poet, essayist, and critic whose work has appeared in *Boulevard*, *American Book Review*, *Pleiades*, and other places. He lives in the Texas Rio Grande Valley.

www.ingramcontent.com/pod-product-compliance
Lightning Source LLC
Chambersburg PA
CBHW022149090426
42742CB00010B/1438